AFTER AMERICA'S
MIDLIFE CRISIS

AFTER AMERICA'S MIDLIFE CRISIS

Michael Gecan

A Boston Review Book

THE MIT PRESS Cambridge, Mass. London, England

MIT Press books may be purchased at special quantity
discounts for business or sales promotional use. For
information, please e-mail special_sales@mitpress.mit.edu or
write to Special Sales Department, The MIT Press,
55 Hayward Street, Cambridge, MA 02142.

This book was set in Adobe Garamond by *Boston Review*
and was printed and bound in the United States of America.

Library of Congress Cataloging-in-Publication Data
Gecan, Michael.
    After America's Midlife Crisis / Michael Gecan.
        p. cm.—(Boston review books)
    ISBN 978-0-262-01360-4 (hardcover : alk. paper)
    1. Social capital (Sociology)—United States. 2. Social
institutions—United States. 3. Education, Urban—United
States. I. Title.
    HN65.G425 2009
    307.74086'9420973—dc22

                                        2009019621

10 9 8 7 6 5 4 3 2 1

To my mother, Mary Gecan

CONTENTS

INTRODUCTION

The Triangle

I DRIVE SOUTH, FROM CHICAGO'S WEST GAR-
field Park into North Lawndale, through a shattered
landscape of dollar stores and vacant lots and an occasional renovated building (New Condos! 75 percent occupied! Going Fast! . . . and largely dark at
night when I drive past, giving "going fast" a mean-
ing the PR people did not intend). It is a landscape
that began to crater more than 40 years ago and
never recovered.

It is December 1, 2008. This afternoon, WGN ra-
dio is reporting that President-elect Barack Obama has
selected Senator Hillary Rodham Clinton as his Secre-

tary of State. It occurs to me that right here, the corner of Madison and Pulaski, is almost exactly midway between Hyde Park, on Chicago's southeast side, and the northwest suburb of Park Ridge. Drive the fourteen miles to Hyde Park, and you will find yourself in the enclave community that the president called home for some seventeen years before taking office. Turn around and drive northwest, you will end up in Park Ridge, where Hillary Clinton was raised before heading off to Wellesley College and Yale Law School.

Think of this as an exercise in social geometry. The announcements of cabinet appointments are all taking place downtown (just miles away from the heart of the West Side) where the other winners in the city and region—the lawyers, developers, real estate interests, and media and public relations elites—congregate. The corporate and civic institutions of downtown, the academic and health institutions of Hyde Park, and the still-thriving bedroom communities of Park Ridge form a triangle. In its center, on Madison and Pulaski, the urban core is widening and collapsing like a toxic asset on a bank's balance sheet. You can spend your entire life in Chicago, moving from one point of the triangle to another and never coming to grips with the reality of this stretch of Madison. And you can spend your entire life here and have no sense of the parallel reality of the people on the commuter trains, at the University of Chicago, or in the office towers downtown. But on Madison is where many Chicagoans—and many Americans—live.

During three summers in the late 1960s, I worked for the Contract Buyers League of Lawndale, led by the late great Monsignor Jack Egan and a determined Jesuit seminarian named Jack Macnamara. Paid ten dollars a week as a junior member of a large and talented staff, I did hundreds upon hundreds of title searches, poring over the plats and maps at Chicago Title and Trust and going half-blind staring at microfilm records.

My colleagues and I read the story of the dismantling of a major part of the city. White families, panicked by real estate speculators, sold low. The speculators' pitch was not subtle. Each night, sometimes in the middle of the night, the phone would ring, and a real estate representative would describe how the coming black buyers would destroy the neighborhood. Often, the caller literally spoke your language—in the case of my family, Croatian.

Once the whites had left, the real estate sharks turned around and sold the same homes at much higher prices to working-class black families. There was a catch, of course: the early version of the adjustable-rate mortgage. Black families, denied normal mortgages by any bank because of their race, had to buy their homes on contract. They had no equity until they made the very last payment. Equity was not earned month-by-month, year-by-year, as in a normal mortgage, but only as a "bonus" at the end of twenty years of faithful and timely payments. Any late payment or short payment meant that they lost everything.

Ruth Wells and Clyde Ross were just two of the thousands of people who faced this real estate gauntlet. Like other Lawndale homeowners, they went to work no matter how sick, no matter how pressed, no matter how worried they were about their teenage kids, because they could not miss a single payment. And because they eventually would, they would find a sheriff on the porch, waiting to evict them. After they met Egan and Macnamara, Wells and Ross emerged as leaders of the group of contract buyers that decided to push back. They picketed the banks that held the mortgages of the sleazy real estate operators. They recruited a top legal team to represent them. They analyzed and documented every transaction in an entire section of the city and proved that there was a clear pattern of abuse and exploitation. Before RICO, they exposed a real estate racket and flushed out the racketeers. They won in court and forced the mortgage companies to reimburse them for their losses.

But the victory, against great odds, was too little and too late. In dozens of other neighborhoods, the racketeers, or their unindicted sons and daughters, went back to work. They kept scamming both the whites who fled and the blacks who came. The dollars that could have gone into home maintenance, home improvement, and tutoring for the kids, went instead to hustlers who worked with the blessing and protection of the Democratic machine. Before long, block after block was bled dry. About half of the neighborhoods of the city started to die.

I remember Lincoln's description, in his second inaugural address, of how "all the wealth piled by the bond-man's two hundred and fifty years of unrequited toil shall be sunk." The longer the evil was tolerated, or ignored, or worked around, the greater the price to be paid by the entire nation "until every drop of blood drawn with the lash, shall be paid by another drawn with the sword." Lincoln's sense of the utter wrongness of slavery was not rooted in visions of racial justice, but in his personal experience with unrequited toil. As a young man, he worked hard and long and gave every dollar earned to his father, who pocketed all of the money. He knew what it meant to live by the sweat of his brow—and to be denied the wage and respect that that sweat should guarantee. He knew there was a steep price to be paid someday by those who exploited and those who condoned the exploitation.

The modern Lawndale version was not slavery, not total, not horrific, not enforced by the lash; but it was marked by relentless labor and modest wages that gave way to slowly losing—seeing stolen—most of what you worked so hard to earn. Your toil was not unrequited when you *did* your work. It was unrequited *over time*. What is the price to be paid for this less-violent, but still brutal and systematic exploitation? When financial institutions will not make loans, when hustlers take full advantage, when political machines make fortunes in the process and get fat, when multiple and bipartisan national administrations enable it all and benefit from it, when the undramatic and generational habits of a people are mocked and the transactional profiteers are celebrated and idolized—what is the *cost* of all of this?

I responded to the world I came to understand by becoming an organizer. I have worked for more than 30 years with colleagues in the Industrial Areas Foundation (IAF), as we found and developed local leaders who sought to build and sustain their communities. When I began, there was still some sense that governmental solutions with a liberal bent could solve many of society's seemingly intractable problems. But that sense was already fading and was swept off the stage by President Reagan's government-is-the-enemy creed and a quarter-century of prayers and incense-burning at the altar of the market. Today, both temples lie in ruins. And, once again, people are watching their lifetimes of work reduced to dust.

Meanwhile, in what Peter Drucker called the "third sector" and what others refer to as civil society, my colleagues and I have carried out many experiments in citizen organizing and social problem solving—some very large in scale, some more local; some clearly successful, some not; and some in too-early a stage to evaluate. These are experiments, often undertaken in partnership with local government, that neither the governmental sector nor the market could or would conduct alone. These experiments have already transformed parts of cities and counties and regions. As conditions for working people continue to deteriorate and as traditional responses keep coming up short, these experiments command greater study.

BEFORE AND AFTER THE RECENT PRESIDENTIAL campaign, the world of organizing was paid an unusual amount attention. After all, the president himself had been an organizer for three years. In fact, he had attended the ten-day training session that my colleagues and I conducted more than twenty years ago. Although he never worked directly with our network, we stayed in touch, on and off, through the years.

Clinton, his most serious challenger, wrote her senior thesis at Wellesley about the IAF's founder, Saul David Alinksy, whose centennial year is now being marked. Alinsky, it is said, offered her a job. She declined, declaring that she believed more significant change would occur within the system, rather than from without.

Even Rudolph Giuliani spent several minutes of his prime time speech at the Republican Convention shining a light—a negative one—on organizing. He pretended not to know what organizing was, or what an organizer did. Giuliani failed to mentioned that as New York City's mayor he spent scores of hours with our groups on a range of critical issues; he attended assemblies, met individually with fifteen leaders, and sought our assistance in times of great crisis. His convention performance backfired, exposing to a national audience his utterly untethered ambition.

Since Obama's victory, many people have asked me if I feel better now that a former organizer is in the White House. They may have been posing a rhetorical question: they assumed I would be thrilled. But I found myself asking another question: where did the three years of organizing experience fit into the overall formation of the president as a public person? And the answer to that question—that the influence of organizing ranked lower than other influences—led to a second question: what were those more formative influences, and what impact would they have on his administration and the nation?

The first influence was one Obama shared with Clinton—the set of relationships, contacts, loyalties and beliefs that began in the nation's elite colleges, law schools, and graduate schools and were reinforced, in public- and private-sector careers ever since. I have written elsewhere that Clinton and many in her political generation:

> left their hometowns and are, in some sense, stateless, even placeless. They weren't formed by decades of party-building, door-to-door voter work, and carefully crafted alliances in a neighborhood or town. To the extent that they are the product of a place, a time, and a people, the place would be college campuses and high-powered law schools. The time would be the late 1960s and very early 1970s. And the people would be other intense college kids, law school students, and political operatives.

This non-geographical tribe places an extraordinary value on academic and other forms of intellectual achievement—as students, as professors, as authors, as opinion leaders. Many members of this tribe care deeply about the issues, particularly the issues of people in great distress. But their caring often expresses itself in sophisticated policies and programs that, conceived from the top down, will almost certainly run afoul of realities on the ground. The best of them, cloistered from the lived reality of most Americans, acknowledge that fact, and try to listen to those who are more closely connected to it. The worst of them have contempt for the experiences of working people and sneer at pragmatic critique of larger policy issues as "anecdotal." The majority, incredibly busy and personally ambitious, is somewhere in the middle. The White House and most federal agencies will be filled with the members of this tribe.

The president is himself an intellectual and an academic. He seems to enjoy the company of the best and the brightest from Stanford and the University of Chicago and Harvard. He kept, cultivated, and expanded his relationships to academics and experts since his days at Columbia and the Harvard Law School. Support for his candidacy surged in part because he communicated to academics that he valued *them*, admired *them*, and would invite them back into the center of power and policy. Academics of all ages were deeply committed to his campaign. They served as leaders and organizers on campuses for him. And they were thrilled by his victory, their joy exceeded only by the pride of the nation's African-American community.

While the newly elected president was mobile as a younger man, and while he shares Clinton's fondness for this tribe of high achievers, he also did something that distinguished himself from her and many others like her: he moved to the south side of Chicago and became rooted in a political culture and a physical place. Here he came under a second strong influence, one that has received little attention in the media. In Chicago, Obama gained for his campaign a key quality that his opponents in the Democratic primaries and the national election lacked: the unparalleled toughness and thoroughness of the Cook County Democratic machine.

When Tip O'Neill—the savvy Congressman from Cambridge, Massachusetts who rose to become speaker of the house—said, "all politics is local," he was talking about the kind of "local" that Cook County officials and machine politicians everywhere understood—neighborhood, ward, borough, precinct, populated by people known both by face and *name*. An effective pol would know where each person worked and prayed, drank and voted.

As most urban machines have rusted and stalled, Cook County's has only become more fuel-efficient. A third generation of Madigans and Daleys, families that first appeared on public payrolls in 1924, now hold a range of powerful offices—mayor of Chicago, assembly speaker, state attorney general. The non-blood family that began with former Chicago city council powerhouse Wilson Frost and continued with former Illinois Senate President Emil Jones adopted a talented and bright young man named Barack Obama. One of the machine's favorite consultants, David Axelrod, played a pivotal role in the presidential campaign. Axelrod had spent much of the previous decade advising Mayor Richard M. Daley. In the transition meetings downtown, William Daley and Rahm Emanuel were major figures—one a blood descendant of the Daley tribe and the other an adopted and adopting son. If you suggested one hundred–year term limits in Cook County, no one in the machine would laugh, and every machine operative would find some reason to object.

The machine is orderly, tidy, predictable, and very tightly connected. The machine is also disciplined. No matter how long your tribe has ruled, no matter how many times you have been elected, no matter how secure your seat, you must pay your respects to its rituals and practices. Robo-calls, email blitzes, or Bruce Springsteen concerts simply will not do. You go door-to-door. You do an exhaustive analysis of every voter on every block in every precinct and ward. You lock up the pluses (sure yes votes) and ignore the minuses (sure no votes). And you focus, with laser-like intensity, on the zeros (the undecideds, the not-yet-determined). You do not trust this work to junior volunteers, or amateurs, or idealists. The machine "don't want nobody nobody sent," as a young and enthusiastic Abner Mikva was told at the beginning of a long and estimable career in public life. This pointed tutorial came from a machine operative who rejected the future Congressman's innocent offer to help in a local campaign.

On the ground, politics is serious business: *the* core, consistent, profit-making business of the city and county. In many campaigns, there are few, almost no, true volunteers. Campaigns are run by reliable pros. And campaign headquarters somehow attract seasoned workers who are paid by the city or county or state. The workers fill every desk at all hours of day and night, and they show up at mid-day by the hundreds, flooding out of government agencies, for "campaign events." These repeated miraculous gatherings of political supporters paid by public agencies, particularly in the few contested elections that occur, rival the apparitions at Lourdes.

During the February primary, I worked on a freezing day at a precinct in Oak Park to try to build support for a Constitutional Convention proposition (opposed by the machine and later defeated soundly). After 30 minutes or so, another worker came over to me and asked, "What clock you on?" At first I did not understand. Then I realized that he was asking who was paying me. "Nobody's clock," I said. He was incredulous. I asked him, "What clock *you* on?" He could not have been more forthcoming. "I work in the city—reviewing architectural plans. That clock. Plus a few others. I make out really great today." Later that night, mired in a sleet storm in the southwest suburbs, I asked another indefatigable machine worker what he was doing. "Passing out cards for some judge," he said. I asked which judge; "How the hell should I know?" he replied. When I pointed to a long Polish name on the cards, the machine worker said, "Yeah, him."

What the president pulled off was remarkable. He mobilized the resources and relationships of both tribes—the non-geographical networks of elite colleges, law schools, law firms, and the like, *and* the most efficient geographically grounded political machine left in the nation. These two groups opposed each other during an earlier age of political reform, lived parallel lives at best, and had very different interests and habits. But they have shared one common experience over more than four decades: both tribes have thrived while the larger worlds around them crumbled.

The academics and professionals who lived in Hyde Park or Evanston, downtown or Oak Park, in Ann Arbor and Madison, in Columbus and Bloomington, in scores of other university enclaves or towns, did very well. The University of Chicago continued to expand and prosper during this period while the president taught at its law school and the first lady worked in a senior management position at its medical center. The northwest Chicago suburb where Clinton grew up remained a pleasant bedroom community for white-collar workers who commuted downtown or to the office parks beyond O'Hare airport. But these bubbles of prosperity were the exception. As Richard C. Longworth has described in *Caught in the Middle*, quality of life in large older cities, indeed the entire Midwest, declined dramatically for most, catastrophically for growing numbers. A 2008 *Milwaukee Journal Sentinel* article noted that the unemployment rate for black men in Milwaukee was over 50 percent.

While the professional tribes were thriving, those who maintained the machine culture of Cook County learned that there was no necessary relationship between political success and social progress. They did not have to deliver decent schools, an honest and effective police force, affordable housing, respectable public housing, and accessible medical care to the majority of their constituents. They did not even

have to protect the working-class white neighborhoods that historically served as the machine's base.
They perfected their control of the West and South
Sides even as population drained and conditions de-
teriorated. Of the scores of bungalow neighborhoods
of lower-middle-class residents, now just a handful
remain. Chicago has lost nearly a million residents
from its population high-water mark in 1947—most
of them white ethnics.

But in return for electoral support, the machine
had two obligations. First, it had to honor the unwritten agreement made decades ago between the
city's mayor and local aldermen. In that agreement,
the mayor got what he wanted on all big decisions—
budget, airports, downtown development, tour-
ism, and the arts—and the aldermen got what they
wanted in their wards. Of course, the local pols then
had to support the machine 100 percent at election
time, and the machine had to protect them from
upstarts and activists who wanted to rock the boat,
or nightmare of nightmares, throw the hacks off the

boat. The unwritten deal had a major downside: a license to steal, a root cause of the endemic corruption in Illinois.

Second, the machine had to keep finding ways to deliver jobs, contracts, favors, and opportunities for profit to its most loyal supporters. Real estate, zoning, insurance, and title work have always been mainstays, as has tax assessment. Private and public colleges, including community colleges with construction and patronage opportunities, have played bigger and bigger roles. Hospitals and medical centers are today's troughs. While there is not much fat in honest-to-god affordable-housing development, the foreclosure business is booming for lawyers, sheriffs, court clerks, and moving companies.

One of the great new growth areas for patronage and profit has been criminal justice and incarceration. In 1970 there were only 7,326 men and women in prison in Illinois. By 2005, there were 44,000. Illinois now ranks 49th in state dollars dedicated to education, while it is near the top of the list in state funding for prisons. In December 2008 the *Chicago Tribune* reported that then-Governor Rod Blagojevich "hired 208 prison guards who don't have a prison to guard." Bruce Western, a Harvard sociologist, writes that the probability of incarceration for young black men such as those on the West and South Sides of Chicago, is now greater than that of graduation from high school.

LIKE THE MAJORITY OF VOTING AMERICANS, I was glad to see the Bush era repudiated. And I have few doubts about the intelligence of the team the new president has assembled. But I worry very much about *their two cultures*—how they have been formed, about how they have prospered while so much of America has faded; how much evil they have tolerated or ignored; and whether they will grapple with deepening and multiplying institutional crises.

There is a chance the president learned some approaches and lessons, skills and tools, from the world of organizing that may prove useful in the years ahead.

Although his organizing tenure is short in comparison to his legal, teaching, writing, or political careers, he might be more open to these lessons than any of his predecessors. But he will also have to fend off the academics who tend to see change only in terms of technocratic policies and who are unable to learn from experience whether the policy actually works. The president will also have to muscle out the machine operatives who could not care less about policies and priorities, but who have perfected the art of transforming all of Washington's money into ever-expanding pools of patronage and local influence.

The effort to restore all that has been lost will be difficult. But the devil is *not* in the details. He's in the large space between policy and patronage—in the muck and mire of implementation, in the netherworld where neither the media nor federal prosecutors tread.

As we say in organizing, the internal fights are always the toughest.

1

On Borrowed Time

IN THE SPRING OF 2008, ABOUT 125 LEADERS from religious institutions, civic organizations, and social service groups met at Etz Chaim synagogue in the town of Lombard, in DuPage County, to wrestle with a new reality: a budget crisis. Budget crises are not supposed to happen in places like suburban DuPage. Cook County's western neighbor is home to nearly one million souls and more than 600,000 private sector jobs. It boasts a median income of $70,000, one of the highest in the nation. And yet the county, strapped for cash, was threatening to cut convalescent services, veterans' services, housing assistance, breast cancer screening, and many other essential public functions.

Until recently DuPage County had been one of the big winners during the 40-year decline and imminent collapse of Cook County. Major corporations fled Chicago's failing downtown and moved to DuPage's open spaces and tax-friendly towns. Working-class homeowners on the West and Southwest Sides of the city sold their bungalows and bought ranch houses, Cape Cods, and new town homes in Wheaton and Naperville and Downers Grove. Families troubled by the city's public schools happily sent their children into shining new facilities and well-equipped classrooms. County government prided itself on its lean budgets and effective service-delivery.

By the date of the meeting, however, the developers who had helped double DuPage's population in just 30 years had run out of land. The income generated by their construction efforts had dwindled to a trickle. Education and public safety costs continued to climb. Scores of specialized local districts and commissions—water, sanitary, and others —absorbed hundreds of millions of dollars that never made it into the general operating budget of the county and were subject to little, if any, scrutiny or oversight. And residential real estate taxes—the backbone of the county's budget due to the long-standing agreement to attract and retain business by keeping commercial taxes low—soared.

The leaders facing the crisis were themselves a new reality—more diverse than anyone would have imagined just ten years ago. In the modern synagogue meeting space, sitting around tables of ten, were approximately fifteen Muslim leaders from mosques and community centers, five Hispanics who were part of an exploding population drawn to the county by plentiful employment, and several African immigrants and African Americans. About one out of four participants were not white—a ratio that represents the make-up of the new DuPage. They were brought together by the leaders and staff of the local Industrial Areas Foundation affiliate called DuPage United.

The organizer of the group, Amy Lawless, asked me to give a 30-minute talk about the state of the county. I started off where I often do, by thinking back to the West Side of Chicago, to the corner of Ferdinand and Springfield near Garfield Park, where my family lived. In the 1950s, there was no way to know that we were living at the city's high point. The massive economic, political, civic, and religious institutions had seemed as solid and stable as glaciers to those living with them or in their shadows. From the second floor of our double-brick corner house, we could see the tavern that we once owned, the then-modern building that housed Newark Electronics, where my father and I would someday work, and the row of houses obscuring the view of Tootsietoy Company, where my mother would be employed. Four blocks north was our parish, Our Lady of the Angels. Children packed its classrooms, and thousands attended Sunday mass.

By the mid-1980s it was all rapidly declining. Today, our home, along with thousands of others, is abandoned. A state social service center fills the old electronics plant. Tootsietoy's products are mostly made in China. And the parish church and school have closed.

In that pleasant synagogue meeting space, with the last of the new McMansions going up across the street, with 60,000 more workers commuting in to DuPage each day than commuting out, with the local football teams on the rise and the SAT and ACT scores still high, I suggested that perhaps the county had hit its own high-water mark and that without clear-eyed re-evaluation, it was poised, as Chicago had been in the mid-1950s, for decline.

DuPage is not alone, of course. In Nassau and Suffolk Counties in New York, in Montgomery and Baltimore Counties in Maryland, in Bergen and Essex and Middlesex Counties in New Jersey, in almost every mature suburb in the Northeast and Midwest and mid-South, families face these same conditions. A Roman Catholic pastor I met in Nassau County described this state of affairs as suburbia's midlife crisis. It may be part of America's midlife crisis as well.

No longer young, no longer trendy, no longer the place to be, no longer without apparent limitations or constraints, these places, like people, have developed ways of avoiding reality.

Denial (supported by ever-stronger doses of public relations). One way is just to deny that there are new realities, or that these new realities will ever affect them. Hundreds of older cities and suburbs, large and small, do this. Denial keeps the real estate crowd happy—selling the safety and schools and jobs of the suburbs, while ignoring the property taxes and rising school and public safety costs, hoping that the younger and fresher and business-hungry counties further west, or the factories of China and tech campuses of India, do not tempt too many companies to leave.

Gimmicks. A municipality buys a soccer team, or minor league baseball franchise, or jai alai fronton, or casino, or all of the above. Bigger municipalities start selling or leasing large parts of themselves. Just two years ago, Chicago leased the Skyway in an attempt to generate revenue and plug holes in an election-year budget. In late 2007 the papers were filled with stories about another $250 million gap. What's the next one-shot? Naming rights are being discussed. And, of course, there is always the summer Olympics of 2016. In a desolate corner of the Near South Side, amid boarded up graystones and eerily empty boulevards during what should be the morning rush hour, a beleaguered local pastor told me that the possibility of an Olympic swimming venue (proposed by the city, for eight years in the future, as part of an Olympic bid with little or no chance of succeeding) would help revive the neighborhood.

Blaming "others." In cities of the 1950s, the "others" were the black workers who had arrived by the hundreds of thousands for jobs that were just beginning to disappear. They needed housing and schools for their children, and the Democratic machine was more than happy to enrich itself by taking money from the developers and real estate hustlers who ran white ethnics out of their neighborhoods and steered minorities in. The political establishment blamed the blacks for the neighborhoods' decline. This extraordinary trope made it possible for a major American city to demolish much of its public housing stock—nearly 18,000 units—and essentially not replace it. Ten years ago these 18,000 families were promised replacement apartments. To date, fewer than 2,000 have been built, most unaffordable to the original renters. When I described this situation to two young and prosperous Chicago businessmen, they expressed no surprise. Blacks *were* the problem, weren't they? And they had to hand it to Mayor Daley for figuring out how to evict them without greater opposition. Today, in the suburbs, the new "others" are immigrants—Hispanic and Muslim. Some blame them for the current fiscal crisis. Meanwhile, the structural, financial, and political challenges of the suburbs—built into their creation and preceding the newest wave of immigrants by three decades—are not dealt with.

Withdrawal: increasing fragmentation and privatization. As the budget crises persist, as the gimmicks become more transparent and inadequate, as the racial and ethnic rhetoric rises, those with resources begin to protect their own interests. Walls of all kinds are built. Private colleges and hospitals will became fiefdoms—supplying their own security, sanitation, even housing at times. Private schools for those who can afford them multiply. Gated communities have become the norm. Most suburbs had little public housing or public transportation to begin with. But the logic for anything "public" will be challenged as revenue to support any shared public activity shrinks. The forces for and against public effort, public institutions, and public life will soon collide in the public schools and public safety agencies of the suburbs.

We have moved a long way from the vision of the nation that Abraham Lincoln described in his Message to Congress, on July 4, 1861: "To elevate the condition of man . . . To lift artificial weights from all shoulders; To clear the paths of laudable pursuit for all; To afford all, an unfettered start, and a fair chance, in the race of life . . ."

Instead, in the Land of Lincoln, the leaders of older cities like Chicago and counties like Cook have already shown how to focus on the few. Their economic strategies have benefited those who own the businesses that cater to the tourist trade, not the workers who make the beds and chop the onions. They have created enclaves around universities and hospitals where parents can buy condos for their student-children and where private security forces patrol the streets. They have sequestered revenues generated by business and medical clusters within those districts, thus starving the larger public housing, health, transit, and educational systems in the sprawling ghettos just outside the gates. They have encouraged construction of homes and apartment towers that few local residents can afford, which are bought as investment by elites. And they have kept control of the courts, jails, and police forces—patronage for the operatives who guarantee machine incumbency—the incarceration industry weakly buffering the loss of the steel and auto and other manufacturing industries of the past.

Many of the paths of laudable pursuit have been closed or semi-privatized—walled, gated, guarded—for some time. For three generations of African Americans, the city and county have been places of a deep and extended depression. For the white-ethnic working class, the results have been more mixed. Hundreds of thousands of families lost equity repeatedly as each neighborhood on the west and south sides was re-segregated. Other whites accepted the instability of repeated neighborhood change for the stability of patronage employment. The city government that put food on the table took money from their savings accounts at Pioneer Bank and Talman Savings and Loan in the form of lost home equity. For more recent immigrants, the city has been stripped of opportunity in some places and sealed off in others.

The Democratic machine and its allies have fought an increasingly costly rear-guard action for nearly half a century. At the end of that period, the image of the city has been burnished, but Chicago is basically broke. Housing abandonment, homelessness, and foreclosure rates are all at historic highs. 34 public school children were murdered during the 2006-7 school year alone. The police force staggers under multiple charges of abuse and corruption. The old bungalow bedrock of the city—blue-collar and tax-paying—has disappeared.

It is instructive to compare Chicago with New York, which seemed in even worse shape 30 years ago. Most Americans remember the famous tabloid headline: "Ford to New York: Drop Dead." As late as the mid-1980s, a major magazine sported a picture of a darkened city on its cover with the letters, "NYC RIP." Indeed, beginning in the late 1970s, the city *was* locked in a very public life-and-death struggle. Only emergency action by labor unions and others saved the city fiscally. But, when faced with municipal mortality—perhaps *because* it had to face its own mortality—a strange thing happened. The city slowly began to revive.

This revival did not start in City Hall or in some political gathering. It was not engineered by a major builder like the legendary Robert Moses. And it was not the brainchild of a great corporate or financial titan. Building began locally, in some of the most forgotten corners of a city that was battling a virulent and advanced form of civic cancer. Renewal began in East Brooklyn and the South Bronx and Manhattan's Washington Heights.

In the late 1970s, a little known group called the Community Preservation Corporation (CPC) began rehabilitating apartment buildings in Washington Heights, one of the drug-ridden areas that Hollywood loved. After 14,000 units were built in a decade, most of the rental housing in the area had been returned to useful life. In 1980 one of our organizations, East Brooklyn Congregations (EBC), began its work in an area that a touring mayor from Boston dubbed, "The beginning of the end of civilization." EBC built 3,000 new, affordable, owner-occupied homes on the vacant acres there, and is constructing 1,500 more as we speak. In the South Bronx, another IAF group, South Bronx Churches, built one thousand homes starting in 1986, while other efforts led by Father Lou Gigante and Mary Daily built or renovated thousands more. Common Ground created 2,000 units of housing for formerly homeless people, giving them shelter, services, and an alternative to the streets. 2,000 more are now in development. Over a 25-year period, more than 200,000 units of housing have either been upgraded or built from scratch. A million New Yorkers have returned to the city, pushing its population back over 8.25 million. The city spent $500 million a year in some years on housing production. In the process, New York transformed lots filled with rubble and tires into neighborhoods for the hard-working families that lived in public housing, but couldn't afford even a starter home in a suburb. Those families held on. They saved. They bought. And they benefited from one of the greatest public works efforts in modern times. Private developers vie for the remaining lots in places like Mott Haven or East New York, where they can now build market-rate housing. This, although still challenging in its own right, was utterly unthinkable in 1980.

During this same period, a similar renewal effort was occurring in public transit. In the 1970s and 1980s, New York City subways were famous for breakdowns, fires, and crime. The number of riders plummeted in what seemed to be a death-spiral. Massive state support, solicited by Richard Ravitch and engineered by the late Speaker of the Assembly Stanley Fink and then-Governor Mario Cuomo, helped stabilize the system. An epic campaign to block the construction of a West Side highway led by Marcy Benstock saved billions for mass transit. Relentless advocacy by Gene Russianoff and the Straphangers Campaign kept the problems and potential of the transit system on the radar screens of the press and politicians. Able management by Robert Kiley meant that the funds raised and saved were put to good use. A workforce of 40,000 transit employees, most of them city dwellers, kept the trains and buses running. Today, breakdowns are rare and crime is remarkably low. Predictably, riders jam the trains and buses at all hours of the day and night. New York is now expanding the subway system by adding spurs and new lines.

Finally, the police department has benefited from the leadership of three mayors over a twenty-year period. David Dinkins secured the funds to hire additional cops. Rudy Giuliani made public safety the hallmark of his administration and hired Bill Bratton to revolutionize police work in the city. And Michael Bloomberg both institutionalized and improved on Giuliani's work, making New York one of the safest big cites and a challenge for the Hollywood crowd looking for edgy street scenes. In 2008 the city recorded 522 homicides—down from 2,250 little more than a decade ago.

These three major improvements—in housing, transportation, and crime—are so large in scale that they are hard to see, absorb, or interpret. Each had a different trajectory and a different character, but they shared some characteristics.

Each was extremely costly, requiring sustained financial support for fifteen years or more. But each long-term investment, once it hit critical mass, also generated extraordinary value. The value of real estate has soared in the toughest and most distant corners of each borough. An NYU study has shown the existing homes near IAF's Nehemiah sites benefited greatly from our construction.

Each improvement took time to build, reach critical mass, and generate a chain reaction in the right direction. The turnaround in public safety has occurred over a fifteen-year period. The renewal of the transit system started nearly 25 years ago. And the revival of the housing stock is in its 30th year, if you count, as IAF does, the work of CPC in Washington Heights as the starting point.

Each improvement was led by a mix of leaders. The overwhelming majority came from the civic or voluntary sector and from the government sector (both elected officials, but, as or more importantly, able administrators in the housing, transit, and public safety fields). The private sector could point to an occasional participant, but, by and large, it lagged the other two sectors by a large margin.

And each improvement was contentious. The leaders involved in these efforts were by no means in sync, cooperative, or even civil to one another. On the contrary, each effort was accompanied by disputes, rivalries, jealousies, and open warfare at times. There was no centralized "meeting of all the stakeholders" in some lavish foundation conference room or elegant university hall.

What to make of this? Even today, the conventional wisdom is that New York is out of control, dangerous, dirty; a nice place to play, but a terrible place to live. And Chicago is tidy, orderly, safe, and a great destination for tourists, business people, and university students. As someone who has lived in and around both cities for nearly 30 years each, I know how hard it is to be objective about them. And stereotypes, once set, often trump reality. Besides, Chicago is the private preserve of the Daley clan, and the current Daley projects all that is positive about the city and takes any criticism of it personally. Chicago has a face and a lakefront focus. New York is no one's personal preserve, not the current mayor's, not the previous mayor's, not the next mayor's. New Yorkers relish their edginess and untidiness, even exaggerate it at times. New York has a blur of faces and multiple points of interest.

One conclusion is that it is better in the long run—as an individual or as a municipality—to face reality. Sometimes, a crisis, such as New York's flirtation with bankruptcy, can help trigger that confrontation. The reality in New York 30 years ago was that both the market and the government had failed miserably—the market unwilling to invest in devastated areas or support a dying city, the government wasting hundreds of millions on do-nothing programs run by local groups connected to hapless pols.

When I described the situation in DuPage County and other areas to a well-respected Republican advisor, he responded in the predictable way: "How about cutting business taxes? Wouldn't that attract commerce and people?" But business taxes have *always* been low in Republican-led DuPage County and are decreasing as a percentage of overall revenue. Even with low taxes, even with 600,000 private sector jobs, even with 60,000 more workers traveling to the county for work than commuting from it, the county finds itself in structural fiscal distress.

When reality is finally and fully faced, it is not all bad. While a whole generation of institutions has declined, a new generation has begun to emerge. In DuPage the Muslim and Hispanic communities are rising and eager to contribute to the next phase of the county's life. Evangelical congregations are thriving all across the country, many arriving at their own mid-life moment after 30 years of astonishing growth. The local community college—the College of DuPage—attracts a diverse cohort of 30,000 students to a single sprawling campus. Vibrant networks created and led by those recovering from alcohol and substance abuse are major presences in almost every urban neighborhood or suburban development. In Long Island, these recovery communities are navigating their ways into the public arena cautiously and creatively. From the most forlorn corners of Chicago's West Side to the packed streets of East Harlem, social entrepreneurs are establishing hundreds of new public schools and public charter schools. In all of these areas, organizations like DuPage United and East Brooklyn Congregations and Washington Interfaith Network and Greater Boston Interfaith Organization are beginning to imagine, design, and implement solutions to what once seemed to all intractable social problems.

A second conclusion is that many of the current political structures and leaders are either unable or unwilling to deal with these new realities. When you find the exceptions, like a reluctantly persuaded but then fully committed Mayor Ed Koch or a housing commissioner like Felice Michetti, fine. But waiting for most to act or blaming them when they do not are often not constructive responses. This puts the burden of thinking and acting back on a new type of civic leader: a volunteer with a real following in a local community, but also with a range of analysis and understanding that crosses town or county or city boundaries. The renewal of most of the failed cities of the failed state of Ohio—Dayton, Toledo, Cleveland, Youngstown, Sandusky, Lorain, and many others—depends on men and women who live in and care about those cities. But they will need to relate to leaders well beyond their own towns. And they will need to become a kind of ad hoc economic strategy team for their area, for their state, and for the struggling Midwestern region.

A third conclusion is that this work will require a new set of allies and partners if it is to succeed. The rebuilding of East Brooklyn depended on the extraordinary leadership and financial support of three religious bodies—the Roman Catholic Diocese of Brooklyn, the Episcopal Diocese of Long Island, and the Missouri Synod Lutheran Church of St. Louis. These three institutions disagreed on almost everything doctrinally, but came together to invest millions of no-interest construction financing to help EBC build affordable housing. Other key allies were the late I.D. Robbins and the current general manager of the effort, Ron Waters. These two construction professionals helped facilitate and oversee the extraordinarily difficult and complex rebuilding effort. Another significant ally was the CPC, which provided invaluable technical assistance and financial support.

Each of these allies was not "local" in the same sense that the East Brooklyn organization was. The local congregational and community leaders had to have the confidence necessary to identify and trust talented people from other spheres. But when they did, they deepened and extended their impact well beyond what anyone could have imagined at the start. A *Harvard Business Review* piece by John P. Kotter describes the need for leaders to "align" the right participants to improve the odds of making major changes. The current alignment of local and national dynastic leadership, tired liberal programs, stale conservative tax policies, and fragmented municipal entities is all wrong. A new alignment—a new generation of local leaders, visionary supporters like the late Bishop Francis J. Mugavero, top professionals in the fields of finance and new business creation, academic talent that is neither too cautious nor on the establishment's payroll—is needed. Better yet, a number of new alignments.

A fourth conclusion is that new kinds of money, from new sources, used in creative ways, will be required if cities, counties and regions are to revive. A relatively modest fund of $8 million, raised from religious sources by EBC in 1982, fundamentally changed the way its proposal to build affordable, single-family homes was received. The group of pastors and lay people from a part of the city that had been designated by the elites for "planned shrinkage" had somehow amassed a sum of money that impressed the mayor, his commissioners, newspaper editors, and developers. That revolving construction fund has generated housing with a current market value approaching one billion dollars. New pools of money—in the hundreds of millions in smaller cities and billions in larger cities and metropolitan regions—will need to be created by these organizations and their allies. Local governments will need to reject the low-tax or anti-tax theology of the post-Reagan era. Higher taxes in support of carefully targeted social and economic strategies will be key to the rebuilding of older American cities and maturing suburbs. During the most productive years of its housing revival, New York City spent more than the next 50 American cities *combined* on housing creation and rehabilitation. It shows. The return on this investment is incalculable.

A fifth conclusion is that there may be a need for less government and more planning. Today, there is as much, or more, local, county, and state legislative activity as ever despite decreasing revenues for fewer and fewer priorities. The virulence of internal disagreements and personal vendettas will only increase as resources disappear. Political disputes will resemble academic battles: more intense because they concern so little. For citizens to continue to spend time and energy in this dynamic is deadly, a slow form of political suicide.

I ended my remarks on a lovely late-October night with a challenge: citizens in suburbs like Du-Page—historically Republican, politically moderate, located between the vast fields and farms that produced the midwest's first phase of prosperity and the once-robust manufacturing center of Chicago that forged the region's second period of wealth—need to align themselves with new leaders from other sectors and cut and clear new paths for peoples' laudable pursuits in the decades ahead. The very act of doing so, of opening these paths, engaging all, figuring out how to offer all people an unfettered start and a fair chance in the race of life, would reinvigorate people and places and position them for the next rich phase of our local and national experience.

2

*New Experiments
for an Old Problem*

IN 1933 MY MOTHER ATTENDED AUSTIN HIGH School, two miles west of the Garfield Park home where I grew up. It was a wonderful school at the time—well-built, well-equipped, and located in an area of substantial homes. If you kept going west, you would end up in the lovely lanes of the first western suburb, Oak Park, whose high school was even more remarkable than Austin. Austin High and Oak Park and River Forest High were part of a broad-based national trend of high school construction and expansion and improved performance. All across America, in big cities, leafy suburbs, and isolated towns, municipalities were building, funding, and running high schools for the children of farmers, construction workers, shopkeepers, factory workers, teachers, bartenders, and the still-small but growing group of white-collar professionals. This slow and powerful shift of institutional tectonic plates below the surface of an entire society is detailed by Claudia Goldin and Lawrence F. Katz in their superb 2008 book, *The Race Between Education and Technology*:

> From 1920 to 1940 the fraction of youths enrolled in public and private U.S. secondary schools increased from 18 to 71 percent. The fraction graduating nationwide soared from 9 to 51 percent.... Mass secondary schooling was indeed a 'remarkable educational movement' and set America far ahead of other nations for decades to come, even the rich European ones. Greater levels of education enhanced economic growth and also led to a more even distribution of benefits.

It also set the stage for the second great institutional shift—the growth of world-class colleges and universities that satisfied the rising demand for additional education. Goldin and Katz argue that the twentieth century could be called the Human Capital Century because these successive institutional movements profoundly altered the American social and economic landscape.

By 1958 the overall performance of students entering American high schools was still unparalleled. But while "the supply of educated Americans increased greatly and almost unceasingly from 1900 to around 1980," there were already signs of serious trouble in many inner-city Chicago schools. Nationally, the high school graduation rate would peak at 77 percent in the 1970s and then dip below 70 percent. High school graduation rates in Europe and other parts of the world caught up and, in some cases, surpassed ours. Austin High School became so dysfunctional that the Chicago Public Schools system finally closed it. The building has recently reopened as the home of several much smaller high schools.

In the course of three-quarters of a century, two institutions—the American public high school and the Roman Catholic school—emerged, expanded, and reached critical mass. The public school movement was truly, in the estimation of Goldin and Katz, grassroots, from the bottom up, and locally owned and driven. Towns and suburbs *wanted* their own high schools and taxed themselves to pay for their construction and operation. Together, these two institutions—operating locally and without coordination—generated a mutually reinforcing chain reaction that produced scores of millions of better-educated and highly skilled Americans. These institutions helped integrate both immigrants and Americans from other parts of the country into the social and economic mainstreams of their new hometowns.

The gross social product of this period is incalculable. Americans for several generations were ready to work—and had living-wage work to do. Some were ready and able to innovate or at least respond to the innovation of others. Most were ready and even eager to read a daily newspaper, maybe several daily papers. Most struggled but were able to begin to lift themselves out of poverty. Many felt they were equipped for a shot at middle-class stability—a three-flat in Austin. (A traditional Chicago three-flat usually housed the owner's family on one floor and renters on the other two.) A few believed they could do even better—a grand rambling Victorian in Oak Park. Then the chain reactions stopped—the Roman Catholic one in 1960 and the public school one in 1975—at least in much of urban America and maybe well beyond.

ON DECEMBER 1, 2008, I WAS IN THE CHICAGO area once more, in the city itself this time, about twenty miles east of the DuPage County synagogue where I spoke in April.

I drove my rented car to the corner of Iowa and Avers, the site of what used to be called the Our Lady of the Angels Roman Catholic School. It was gray and cold; not unlike the day, exactly 50 years before, when the old building that used to dominate the intersection caught fire. Ninety-five people—92 children and 3 nuns—died.

Today, the corner was empty and quiet. There was no billowing smoke, no continuous wave of alarms and sirens, no mayhem—firemen, parents, nuns, children, priests, reporters, bodies—on the sidewalks and streets. And there were no gatherings, no prayer vigils, no media. There had, however, been a memorial service the day before at a church many miles away. And the newspapers, particularly the Sunday papers, reported the anniversary extensively. One reprinted the Sunday edition of the *Chicago American*, its front page covered with the faces of the children who died.

I was there that day, a nine-year-old, in the fourth-grade class lucky enough to be located on the first floor. When we heard the fire alarm late in the after-noon, we groaned at the thought that dismissal that day would be later than usual. Fifty of us stood and began to march from the room. Sister Mary Edgar had written the assignment for that night in her elegant script on the blackboard: "Geography, read page . . . ." When we left the room, we noticed the smoke, thick as muscle, massing on the stairwell. This was no poorly timed fire drill.

Most Chicagoans of a certain age can remember where they were, what they were doing, and how they responded to the news of the fire, just as they can remember the moment they heard that President Kennedy had been assassinated. Fifty years later, whenever I hear the sound of a fire truck, or see or smell smoke, or watch a child walk into a dingy school, or hear a public or church official deflect accountability, I am reminded of that afternoon. On September 11, 2001, as I sat in my car on the packed New Jersey Turnpike, I had a sense of what was happening just ten miles away, could see again the walls of the school, with the ladders brought by the nearest neighbors and desperate parents of Our Lady of the Angels, ladders too short to reach the upper floor windows where children and sisters were dying.

The inquest that followed revealed that, because the school was built before the 1949 municipal code went into effect, it was not required to comply with the updated standards regarding overcrowding. Everyone in authority—the city, the archdiocese, the fire department—knew that only 232 students should have been in the six classrooms on the second floor, not the 329 who packed those rooms on the day of the fire. In addition, the delayed call to the fire department was traced to the fact that the nearest firebox was a block and a half away, not the one hundred feet from the school that the updated municipal called for. For nearly ten years before the fire, those in charge were aware of the risks and never bothered to act on behalf of the children and sisters.

I stopped near the school—closed by the Roman Catholic Archdiocese and now operating as a much smaller charter school—and reflected for a few minutes. The church, also closed by the Archdiocese, was now the home of New Miracle Temple Church. The former rectory, hunched between what once was a large school and a still-massive church, now housed the Mission of Our Lady of the Angles—a Catholic outreach on the West Side of Chicago. That meant that there was a priest attempting to minister to people in the area, but essentially no congregation. Stone slabs—not much bigger than many headstones at St. Adalberts Cemetery—engraved with the names of those who died in the fire were erected in the small yard between the rectory and the street 49 years after the event.

I toured the old neighborhood that afternoon. Down Hamlin to Ferdinand, across Ferdinand to Springfield, 3857, where our family lived. My grandparents moved there in the 1920s, with their goods in a horse-drawn wagon. The house, well-built, double-brick, right on the corner, was converted into a small pentecostal church in 2003 and then abandoned. It seemed to be occupied again. The homes across the street were all gone. The tavern that my parents ran two blocks away was now a parking lot.

For me each home or lot still had a name. Belan. Orlando. Tomasovich. Alcala. Sullivan. Stamper. Palmisano. Przybylo. Golich. Wise. Stepkovic. Labbe. Furlan. Whitaker. Juric. Czechs. Italians. Croatians. Irish. Poles. One Mexican family who lived right nextdoor. One West Virginian family who somehow settled in our midst. One African American family at the end of the block whose name I never knew.

Our parents sent us—1,600 of us—to the local parish school and trooped faithfully in even greater numbers—mothers and fathers and aunts and uncles and grandparents—to Mass every Sunday. The huge parish church, where I served Mass, was always packed. As an altar boy, I had to fight the tendency to pass out—not from the incense, but from the relentless press of people.

And ours was just one school and one parish among a dozen or so on the West Side, where hundreds of thousands of Roman Catholics sent more than ten thousand of their boys and girls to parochial schools. When the West Side began to change racially in the late 1960s, these families were replaced by African Americans, most of whom were fleeing worse conditions in the tenements east of Garfield Park or the hallways of the Henry Horner Homes. These were all what used to be called "working-class people," when "working class" was still an acceptable phrase to use, when the notion of being defined by the word "work-ing" was not just descriptive, but somewhat positive. The whites who sent their kids to school and put quarters in the envelope and attended the Holy Name Society smokers were hard workers. Like my father, many earned their livings in factories and plants and railroad yards, where muscle and sweat were part of every day's work. And the blacks who replaced them in these bungalows and two-flats were the same—had the same values and aspirations and anxieties—but lacked the institutional support that places like Our Lady of the Angels provided. Or, to put it another way, Our Lady of the Angels never saw the new families as people to welcome, engage, convert, recruit. So both church and neighborhood perished.

The years right before and after 1958 were the high-water mark of Roman Catholic educa-tion—and perhaps Roman Catholic parish life as a whole—in the United States, though no one knew it at the time. In 1960 Roman Catholic schools were educating more than 5 million students in 13,000 campuses. While the post–World War II years saw the greatest gains, the system had been expanding since 1920. In hundreds of urban areas like Chicago's West Side, Roman Catholic schools gave families with limited means a choice. They provided healthy competition for the nearby public schools and also relieved the pressure on them. While their quality varied, the best of these schools helped lift millions of families out of poverty or near-poverty into lives of economic stability.

Today there are fewer Roman Catholic schools—7,955—than there were in 1920. And these schools followed the second and third generation of ethnic Catholics to the suburbs. At least two generations of young West Siders have grown up in a place of accelerating decline and increasingly scarce educational resources. The educational options they have had—shrinking Roman Catholic institutions and struggling public schools—have all been of poorer quality than the schools my generation knew. Of course, the neighborhood was not perfect: it had its

pathological killers, too; its mobsters and their wan-
nabes; its habit of fighting any outsider. And, if we
ran out of outsiders, we fought one another.

The level of violence was always high, and has
only risen. As 2008 came to a close, homicides in
Chicago—most occurring on the West and South
Side streets like the ones near Our Lady of the Angels—topped 500.

Six weeks after my visit to the old neighborhood, on a frigid but brilliant Sunday in January,
I stopped by New Miracle Temple at 11 a.m., the
time of its Sunday service.

I had not been inside the church itself for nearly
40 years, not since my parents moved to Division
and Menard in the deteriorating Austin area and,
seven years after that, five miles further north to
a tiny home on Central Avenue near Bryn Mawr,
where total racial change and plummeting property
values could never reach them again. At least, that
was their hope. With each move, they lost equity and

fell further behind economically. At age 60, after two lifetimes of grinding work in factories, construction sites, a family tavern, the back office of a toy company, and other jobs, they had no savings. They had worked all week and gone every Saturday morning by bus to Pioneer Bank on North Avenue to make a deposit. Then they bought homes and lost most of their investment in them when their neighborhoods changed. Multiply this experience by the hundreds of thousands in Chicago alone, by many millions in the nation.

(It is important to recall that this cyclical build-up and loss of savings and equity took place during a time when Americans habitually and doggedly *did* save. The personal savings rate of Americans "hovered around 9 percent" right up to the mid-1980s, according to *New York Times* economics columnist David Leonhardt. "In the late 1980s, however, the rate began to fall. In the 1990s, it averaged only 5 percent. In the last several years, it has barely exceeded zero," he wrote in October of 2008.)

Three teenage boys were horsing around in front of the church. As I, an older white man in an overcoat and tie, headed up the steps, they stopped and eyed me. *Who's this guy?* I pushed open the large doors and walked in. An elderly deacon greeted me with a smile, "Morning. Welcome. God bless." I asked if I might go inside the church and sit for several minutes, just pay a visit. He said I was most welcome—for a few minutes or the entire service, any day, anytime.

Inside, about twenty people had gathered. A young man, maybe twelve, sat at the drums on the altar. A keyboardist was settling into his seat and making some adjustments. Great drapes hung from the ceiling 40 feet above, cutting the length of the sanctuary in half and hiding the rear of the church from from the apse and front pews. I could see why. Fully open, the church would seat over a thousand people. The portion sectioned off could seat 400 or so. About ten more people filtered in over the next few minutes, then five more, bringing the congregation, at 11:15 a.m., to 35.

I served hundreds of Masses in this church, learned Latin that I did not yet understand but could readily recite, and followed the priest as he led the congregation in the Stations of the Cross. Just to my left, the words, "Jesus falls the third time," were still visible. On the afternoon of the fire, we were all brought into this space, 1,500 frightened kids, without coats, so close to the school we could hear the windows shattering, the sirens wailing, the shouts and thuds and cries just a few yards away. One of the sisters ordered us to kneel and pray. Some friends and I disobeyed—no small thing, slipped out of the pews, and ran outside.

On those heartbreaking and confusing Sundays after the fire, I sat with my parents and sister and our grieving neighbors and tried to pray, tried to understand. As months and years passed, we all pretended to return to normal. Every Saturday, like all the kids in the neighborhood, I came here and lined up at one of the confessionals to reveal my sins under the sun-charged stained-glass windows of Saints Philip,

Bartholomew, John, Thomas, and James the Minor. One of the confessionals was now the media center for the church, with sound and light consoles all neatly arranged.

The music began, and the congregation rose and sang the opening hymn. It is no exaggeration to say that 35 Evangelical members and one guest sang with more gusto than a thousand Catholics once did in this same space. The Bishop Perry Williams, Jr. and three female associates—one, I guessed, his wife—led the singing. The drummer was one of the best twelve-year-old musicians you will ever hear. It strikes me that there is not much difference between a twelve-year-old ethnic Catholic kid, responding in Latin, leading a procession, and helping conduct services for one congregation and a twelve-year-old African-American Evangelist kid, pounding away at the drums in front of this smaller audience. The church, in both cases, is opening the door to public life and giving the time and space to rehearse, so to speak, for other arenas in our lives.

On my way out, I chatted with the deacon for a few minutes. I told him that this had been my parish more than 50 years ago and that I appreciated the hospitality. He said that the congregation had been in this building twelve years. I said that it seemed like a lot of building to maintain. He continued smiling, but he nodded. He did not want to complain. Then, almost under his breath, he said, "The basement does stay flooded." It is not hard to imagine the many troubles that a vibrant, but small, congregation must face thanks to an aging sanctuary, neglected for the last twenty or more years of its existence as a Roman Catholic facility, suited for thousands, not scores. I was buttoning my coat and heading for the door when he asked, "Were you in that fire?"

I walked the neighborhood for a while. The Galapagos Charter School—all 270 students and staff—occupies a portion of the "new" school building constructed after the fire. This building once teemed with six times that number. A sign on the grate that has been pulled down over the front door reads: "Accepting applicants for K-6 Grades." The overhead and maintenance costs of a building this size, like the church 30 yards away, can overwhelm a smaller institution, no matter how vital, that is just trying to stabilize and grow. Diagonally across from the school is a large vacant lot with a faded "For Sale" sign on it. The blocks around the church and school are pocked with these empty lots, a few boarded up homes, and very worn and aged bungalows and two-flats. Every one of these houses was once filled with people—larger families, sometimes two or even three generations per structure, and so many kids that they packed all the public and Catholic and other schools in every direction. It is still cold, but not so cold as to keep kids from playing. Yet the streets are still.

Chicago Avenue, a block south, is a dreary run of chicken shacks, hair salons, and storefront churches. Young guys in hooded sweatshirts, like modern monks, are working the corners—eyes on the light traffic, waiting for a car to pull to the curb and a customer to make a buy.

WHILE I CANNOT VOUCH FOR THE QUALITY OR staying power of the public charter school in the former Our Lady of the Angels, I do know that the West Side is home to a quiet transformation in education.

If you look closely, you will find many new start-up or reorganized schools in the area. The Jesuits already run a Cristo Rey high school in the Pilsen area to the southeast. The Cristo Rey school attracts Hispanic students, and the Jesuits have just launched another high school in Austin that will primarily serve the African American community. The Christian Brothers have begun several San Miguel middle schools in the vicinity of the new Jesuit high school, with some of the young teachers housed in a communal setting in an apartment building nearby. A group of young and dedicated lay leaders, with Jesuit connections, have started a new Nativity elementary school. Outside of Cristo Rey, most of these new Roman Catholic efforts are start-ups, serving hundreds of students, not thousands. But there is great promise here.

Perhaps the most successful and stablest of the new schools in the area is North Lawndale Prep, a public charter school that opened in 1998 and serves nearly 700 students. Its graduation rates and other statistics rival schools in wealthy suburban districts twenty miles to the north and west. While North Lawndale Prep is fully public and non-religious, at least one of its founders is a former Roman Catholic priest who left the priesthood decades ago, married, and channeled his ministry into the founding and administration of a great school in one of the nation's toughest neighborhoods.

The emergence of what may become a new generation of schools out of the rubble of the West Side reminds me of a talk that the Reverend Johnny Ray Youngblood gave to 8,000 leaders on a vacant lot in East Brooklyn in the late 1980s, when it was still too soon to know if New York City would ever rebuild and revive. Reverend Youngblood was one of the top leaders of EBC, which had already built hundreds of affordable homes and was preparing to build thousands more. On a brilliant Sunday afternoon, Reverend Youngblood told the crowd, "We're not grassroots. Grassroots are shallow roots. Grassroots are fragile. They die. We're deeper than that and stronger than that. Our roots had to push through the broken glass and rubble." And through the cynical politicians. And the "progressives" who thought they had the answers. And the reporters who could not find their way to a neighborhood that had almost literally been burned and bulldozed and neglected off the map.

The growth of these new schools shares some of the characteristics that define the physical rebuilding of East Brooklyn and other forgotten corners of New York. The effort is highly decentralized and varied, with responsibility spread among many individuals and institutions. Religious, public charter, and public school leaders often operate independently, sometimes unaware of or unrelated to one another, sometimes wary.

The activity is highly entrepreneurial, with determined leadership provided by former Jesuits who worked in Lawndale 30 and 40 years ago, by lay leaders in their late-twenties who want to make a difference, by business leaders who are looking for ways to contribute to society, by local ministers seeking to create a new generation of anchor institutions in communities left for dead, by parents who dream of a better life for their kids, and by the kids themselves, donning shirts and ties and responding to the care and discipline of a new kind of school.

This growth is highly localized and almost obsessively focused, with each school team locked into the families and struggles on the blocks around their schools. Maximum effort is required.

It is a long-term commitment. The West Side may be becoming a kind of incubator of new schools of all kinds. The best are not just delivering good teachers and curricula; they are trying to create a culture—habits and patterns, tools and beliefs—of teaching and learning that will last a lifetime.

But their successes are still fragile and will be vulnerable to threats for years to come. The first is the sagging economy that could slow down critical fundraising initiatives just as some of the schools are starting to expand.

Another threat is the academic and legal tribes' tendencies to over-centralize and over-coordinate. Schools and their leaders need time and space to start, experiment, fail, refocus, and expand. This kind of activity happens most effectively when policy operatives and bureaucrats exercise restraint and respect local enterprise. Leaders of these schools have little or no time for umbrella groups, endless meetings, or interference from other arenas. They need to recruit and train young teachers, to remove teachers who cannot make the grade, to provide remedial instruction for students who have had poor instruction at previous schools, to find and renovate facilities, to raise money, and more.

A third threat is interference from elected officials who have had little to do with the establishment and success of many of these schools. If the schools continue to expand, the pols will naturally see them as potential sources of patronage or other forms of support, or as the possible breeding ground of opposition and competition. Most schools now maintain civil relationships with local pols, but too much interference would be fatal.

A fourth threat is the temptation to become too programmatic and reductive at an early stage. The attempt to make all educational efforts conform, or to fit these unique experiments into a single formula, would cause great harm.

To date, thankfully, the Chicago political leadership has done no such harm, and perhaps even some good here.

It is true that these endeavors do not yet offer the opportunities for profit or patronage that housing development, health clinics, and many other public functions provide.

It is true that the local teachers union—an American Federation of Teachers branch—has been inept and corrupt and incapable of mounting an aggressive defense against this new school formation.

It is true that the reason so many public schools are closing and consolidating is that the machine refuses to build replacement affordable housing in the neighborhoods the schools serve, thus reducing population and increasing the costs of maintaining huge, half-filled and heat-leaking buildings.

It is true that the movement to create religious and other private schools relieves the public system of a responsibility and harmonizes with two tendencies of recent years. One is to resist attempts to build replacement affordable housing in any volume, hoping against hope that gentrifiers with full wallets and empty nests will surge west and link up with the Starbucks of Oak Park someday. This tendency means that the student populations of West Side neighborhoods continue to decline, the cost of maintaining half-empty schools keeps rising, and the rationale for closing or consolidating them grows stronger. The second tendency is to offload more and more formerly public functions— from the Skyway to Midway Airport to parking meters—to private and nonprofit operators.

And it is true that the same Chicago machine that botched or corrupted so many other activities has not yet botched or corrupted this one. In fact, two of the most able people in the city ran the Chicago Public Schools system until recently. Arne Duncan was its C.E.O. until he was tapped to be the Secretary of Education in the Obama Administration. And Hill Hammock, the Schools' chief administrative officer, assisted Duncan during this period. Hill, too, is now gone. Ominously, the mayor selected Ron Huberman, an unfailing Daley and Democratic machine loyalist, to replace Duncan.

The alternative-schools movement offers a hint of how to rebuild neighborhoods that have declined for almost two generations. With a growing number of new or reorganized schools, it now makes sense to renovate apartments near those schools and rebuild the blocks around them with truly affordable homes. It also makes sense to consider rehabbing apartment buildings that can serve as communal homes for young teachers and administrators, with their housing opportunity perhaps included in their wage and benefit package. With new schools comes the opportunity to renovate fields and athletic facilities in the vicinity of these schools and to attract a top-flight teacher-training program to the area, so teacher candidates can train in schools alive with new educational opportunities and experimentation. In fact, it is possible to think of the West Side—sizable, perhaps four miles north to south by six miles east to west—as an extended campus. It would be anchored on the east by the University of Illinois at Chicago and would extend all the way to the Oak Park and Cicero borders on the west. Forget about the notion of some vague "village" raising the child. It takes a large area—a mini-city of almost 200,000 residents and 40,000 school-age children, where a commitment to the growth and development of youngsters becomes the widely accepted and adopted and implemented mission of parents, teachers, school leaders, students, pastors, and others.

And Chicago is not the only place, not even the leading place, where signs of new life are emerging.

Twenty years ago, IAF organizations began trying to generate improvements in chronically failing public high schools in Brooklyn and the Bronx. We went to private employers and private colleges and universities and persuaded them to promise jobs or scholarships to students in the high schools who maintained good grades and met other criteria. The effort struggled from the start, in large part because the so-called professionals in the schools had no faith in the students they were teaching. In fact, the culture of the schools was based on the assumption that the students could not succeed, that they were a bundle of "special needs" that could only be met by an endless supply of well-funded, over-staffed, unaccountable social programs.

Then, one terrible afternoon, a student shot and killed two fellow students in one of these high schools, Thomas Jefferson High, in Brooklyn. A third student, a bystander, went home and committed suicide the same day. In the aftermath of this cataclysm, a few days after one of our congregations buried one of the victims, we met with the schools' chancellor and said that we could not reform these failing schools. We proposed what was then considered a new and different response—the creation of smaller high schools that we would cosponsor with the city school system. These schools, we predicted, would be safer, academically superior, and capable of creating a more positive culture for professionals, students, and parents. They would attract talented school leaders who would not have to serve deadly apprenticeships under senior principals who only dream of retirement. They would be welcoming to energetic younger teachers coming out of graduate school with vision, commitment, and the kind of work ethic scorned by burned-out veterans and union hacks. The schools would be small enough to foster relationships among staff and students and parents: overwhelming scale could not serve as an excuse for poor performance or lack of accountability.

There are more than 270 such schools in New York City—public schools—educating about 70,000 students. There are another 80 or so public charter schools attended by some 25,000 youngsters. Many of these schools perform at very high levels. Some have failed. A few have been closed and reorganized. This is all to the good. Schools, even ours, should be closed if they fail. They should not be supported perpetually at increasing cost. Yet, while there have been setbacks, a set of schools educating almost one hundred thousand New Yorkers in novel ways, does exist. Unto themselves, these alternative institutions comprise a system that is larger than most other school systems in the nation. And the system has grown thanks to a remarkably consistent and powerful push from organizations like ours, with mixed cooperation from the old and dysfunctional and often corrupt former New York City Board of Education, with both opposition and grudging acceptance from one of the most powerful unions in the city, and with strong support from the re-centralized Department of Education and a mayor who has had full control.

In New York the same children who were once written off by professionals are succeeding today. A culture that said failure was the fault of the student and family and community has been challenged by a culture that blames failure primarily on the professionals who have not measured up. Many of the remaining, larger, public schools in the city have shown improvement—in part because of the constructive pressure created by the newer, smaller schools, in part because some of these schools have been reformatted to house three or four smaller institutions, and in part because the expectation of higher performance has begun to permeate professionals in all corners of this vast public system of more than one million students and 1,300 schools.

In both New York and Chicago, we may be witnessing modern versions of the movement described by Goldin and Katz that characterized the country for the first three-quarters of the last century. The movement's leaders understand that the time frame for start up and success is extended—ten years or more for a firm start, twenty years or more for mature development. And space—physical space, new and upgraded facilities—is critical. Government must defend these start-ups from itself—from the bureaucrats and politicians who would interfere or enforce conformity. The entire development must be protected from the tendency of the right to think that market privatization (Vouchers! Bust the unions!) is the answer. And it must be defended from the tendency of the left to assert its own ideological demands (Watch out for religion! Everything must be union! Turn everything into a government program!). There are threats on all sides to an effort that is, at bottom, based on a spiritual (though not necessarily religious) belief in the ability of all young people to learn and grow and thrive. But if this movement can continue, if the threats can be deflected, and if the conditions can be created to support this kind of initiative more broadly, we have one answer to the larger question of how we rebuild the West Side and all the West Sides of the nation out of the ashes of the past 40 years.

THE TEACHERS ATTRACTED TO NEW AND IMPROVING schools in Chicago and New York are a small part of a potentially vast pool of workers who may represent a second answer to our question. They did not pick their profession, or return to it, to be supervisors or paper pushers, or to put in time until vested for their pensions. They imagined themselves working with people; helping people; making a meaningful contribution to a student or fellow teacher, a parent or neighborhood. They knew that the quality and impact of their work, and the satisfaction they would derive from it, would result from the daily act of relating directly to the individuals and families others would call their customers. So they understood that the medium may not *be* the message, but the development of a public relationship best guarantees that the message will be delivered. The relational medium is the all-important infrastructure that makes the movement of ideas and values and traditions possible and mutual.

If you asked most of them who they are or what they do, they would answer with the word *teachers* or *educators,* which of course they are. At IAF we use the term *relational workers* and believe that all good teachers are part of this broader group. While information is important to what teachers do and who they are, they are not, in our view, primarily what Drucker dubbed knowledge workers. Nor do they fit into the other major category Drucker described: service workers; although provision of a service is part of what they do. They represent a third major type of worker, whose success or failure at imparting knowledge or delivering a service depends on the ability to build and maintain a sustained relationship with others.

The late Bernard Crick approached this theme from another direction in his superb short book, *In Defence of Politics*. He talked about the "affirmative individual" *and* the need for human institutions created by and for those individuals. He called this generating of social institutions "the natural wealth of corporate life." His book details why every totalitarian culture—left-wing, right-wing, market, machine—

seeks to crush or co-opt that natural wealth. In Crick's view, most people, most of the time, will do the right thing if given the opportunity. Not all people; there are some very bad apples. Not most people all the time; we all fail or fall short at times. And very few people, *if not given the opportunity.* Still, on balance, we are not only capable of good but ready to enact it. Although Crick was secular, he articulated a form of faith in human nature and human development. And he put the right kind of burden on adult society: to create the educational and political conditions and institutions that enable most people to express fully their fundamentally affirmative natures.

The men and women working in small, new schools and older, reorganized schools, from Chicago's West Side to East Brooklyn and the South Bronx, are working in the spirit of Crick and Lincoln. The remarkable relational work these committed teachers perform seems almost quaint when compared to the wealth amassed, until recently, by hotshot investment bankers, or the perks and profiteering opportunities available to high-level political and lobbying opera-tives throughout the United States.

But perhaps the lasting value of this relational work, as one of the few remaining pillars of a col-lapsing economy, has become more apparent in re-cent months. As Longworth wrote in *Caught in the Middle*:

> Basically, any job that does not require face-to-face contact with a customer can be outsourced. Defense attorneys who must appear in court cannot be in India, but real estate lawyers searching titles can. An Indiana X-ray technician has to be in the same room with the patient; the doctors who read the X-rays can be any-where. Barbers in Columbus, taxi drivers in Chicago, and kindergarten teachers in Des Moines are outsource-proof. Stockbrokers and tax accountants aren't. All this is happening now.

Longworth wrote this well over a year ago, and he is more right today than he was then. We can also turn this thought around: any job that *requires* face-to-face contact with another person can be preserved and improved and even expanded.

Unfortunately, even at this very late date, we have hardly developed the language to convey what lies at the core of good relational work, which I discussed several years ago in my book, *Going Public*. Relational work is not essentially technical or bureaucratic. It is a craft that depends on high standards, some recognized masters, a process of apprenticeship, and a commitment to ongoing evaluation and improvement. It *assumes* a basic respect for the materials of the trade—in this case, the lives of students, patients, tenants, citizens. These people cannot be seen as clients, or metrics, or worse. Relational work is essentially, almost radically, reciprocal: student and teacher, nurse and patient, cop and citizen—all *need* one another for long term success and real satisfaction. And it is authoritative: it embodies traditions that have been refined and have stood the test of time. The best practitioners do not just have *knowledge*; they have *judgment*; and the best of the best have wisdom.

We lack the language in part because the institutions that once sustained and advanced a relational culture have declined. The neighborhoods of the West Side were dense networks of overlapping relationships—at the plant, at the union hall, at the corner tavern, at the Holy Name smoker, at the Altar and Rosary Society, on the buses and Els, on the streets and stoops. And the sister who stood in front of the classrooms of Our Lady of the Angels School knew each of us, our brothers and sisters, our parents and friends. But the leaders of those institutions, at some point, lost focus. They took for granted that faithful ethnic immigrants would keep filling the pews and desks and coffers. The people needed a church and school more than a church and school needed the people. For whatever reason—pinching pennies? wishful thinking? a pass from the fire inspectors or local alderman?—these authorities of the civic life thought an extra hundred kids on a crowded second floor and a call box a block and a half away were not worth worrying about. Only, in this case, their loss of focus was fatal. And their neglect made national and international news.

At the same time, we do not yet have enough new or replacement institutions that recognize the radically relational nature of effective ministry and teaching and learning. In the religious world, the percentage of people who identify with a specific denomination or faith continues to decline. That decline has several causes, but the greatest contributor, in my view, is not technological expansion or changes in the way people live and behave. Flocks are thinning because religious institutions no longer relate as persistently and meaningfully to their members and potential members as they once did. Many Evangelical congregations—large, yet often compulsively relational—are exceptions to this rule.

Schools of higher learning, too, rarely construct their curricula or design their apprenticeship efforts with relational goals in mind. Instead, schools of public policy try to outdo one another by teaching arcane mathematical formulae. In most seminaries, there is an understandable emphasis on languages, theology, and preaching, but almost no preparation for meeting individuals, preparing basic analyses of the public relationships among the congregations' members, or locating the congregation on the map of the local community or city or town. The most basic relational tools and practices are either totally ignored or given very short shrift. (Notably different is Drew Seminary in Madison, New Jersey, which offers students a five-day, intensive training session focused on the craft of public relations.) In the majority of teachers' colleges, the students are measured and advanced according to their ability to absorb mostly meaningless and often highly theoretical material and to endure long enough to amass the required number of credits. They often leave these schools almost totally unprepared in the only two areas that matter: a love and mastery of their subject and an understanding of how to relate effectively to their future students and their students' parents.

Finally, the system of rewards and incentives is completely upside-down. Those who spend their lives doing vital relational work should receive pay increases, promotions, and recognition because of the quality of the work and because they remain in relationships with others. The higher-paid workers should be the ones still in the local classroom, or primary health care center, or local police precinct. Instead, the system in almost every profession offers greater rewards and higher status to those who move away from their constituents—into management, into supervision, into consultancy work, into executive director positions. In fact, money and status increase the further one moves from directly relating with students or parents or patients or customers. Instead of protecting relational workers from bureaucratic distraction—worship of turf and technology, unnecessary paperwork and administration—most institutions place a higher value on those who run the bureaucracy and rise to its top.

In short, our nation's organization of public work and public workers is every bit as outdated, top-heavy, and bankrupt as the old Soviet Union. It is layered with patronage people who do little or no real work and who advance either by political fix or automatic bureaucratic promotion. This culture consumes staggering amounts of human and financial resources, with states such as New Jersey supporting hundreds of local school districts, some with very few students, a few with *no* students. Even the districts with no students have highly paid superintendents.

In this time of crisis, there may be an opportunity to reexamine and revalue relational work, to redesign the ways these workers are prepared and trained, and to reorganize the system of rewards and incentives surrounding this work. Every other reform—to our larger school systems, our health care systems, our welfare and incarceration systems—will be undermined if we fail to do this now. Without a better-prepared and better-supported set of relational workers, our policy discussions about important public matters will continue to be played out as endless and exhausting duels between non-relational liberal programs and non-relational conservative tax cuts. These dueling abstractions miss the critical players as well as the dramatic moment of all lasting social change: when a skilled relational worker and a fellow citizen meet.

A new culture of preparation should be created in another institution that needs retooling and reorganization—the American community college. Forty years ago, a handful of scattered vocational schools began to multiply and grow into what is now a vast and sprawling educational reality. More than 45 percent of American college students attend a community college. Community colleges are a major employer and presence in hundreds of counties, and an increasingly desirable and affordable stepping stone toward a college degree.

But community colleges often try to do too many things and lack the commitment to preparing students in the relational arts and skills necessary to be more effective in their careers. The training, apprenticeship, and mastery programs needed to prepare American relational workers should be available as specialized community college offerings. These courses, if well-designed, would attract hundreds of thousands of students from other countries interested in learning these same skills and using these same tools. A nation that once led the world in the production of commodities and cars and appliances can now lead the world in the "production" of top-flight teachers, school leaders, social workers, cops, housing managers, ministers, coaches, substance abuse workers, and many other relationship-based careers.

These workers and this work represent a rich and remarkable resource. At their best, they create and nurture the kinds of vital institutions and affirmative individuals fundamental to a healthy society. These workers serve as social knitters, stitching a community and a city and a country together, making each greater than the sum of its separate pieces. As a group, they are as precious as wetlands, as valuable as oil. But, like wetlands and oil, they take time to mature and develop. They can be damaged or squandered. Their presence can be taken for granted. Their depletion is gradual and subtle, but catastrophic. And they are very difficult, once lost, to replace.

3
A Fair Start

WE HAVE AT LEAST TWO MAJOR PROBLEMS AS we struggle through the current economic catastrophe—the most serious crisis to face us since World War II.

The first is that the policy structures and political tribes that now dominate—Republican and Democratic, tax-cutting and program-generating, corporate and labor—have little or no application to or experience with the kinds of challenges that need to be addressed if we are to rebuild both our social and economic capital in the next generation. They matured in prosperous corners of a declining world—the Ann Arbors, Princetons, and Palo Altos—and kept managing the damage felt by ever-increasing numbers of Americans.

At the local level, where scarcity reigned, where opportunities were few, where the sons and daughters and grandsons and granddaughters of local pols had no other career path or skills, elected and appointed officials have increasingly resorted to corruption or nepotism or both. Both locally and nationally, many of the structures and people who exercise power do not see it in their interest to operate differently. If they play offense, it is the kind of abstract and disconnected offense that those too far away from reality draw up and run. More often, especially locally, they play tougher and meaner defense. They see the world shrinking all around them. They fight harder to keep a grip on what little they have.

The second problem is that most of the instruments that society still uses to fix social problems no longer work. Job retention programs try to retain jobs that began to disappear decades ago. Job training programs most often train people for jobs that no longer exist or that exist in very few numbers. Twice a week, I park my car near the Grove Street station of the PATH line in Jersey City, then take the train into the World Trade Center stop in Manhattan. Each time, I walk past the Jersey City Employment and Training office. IAF's New Jersey group, Interfaith Community Organization, exposed this agency as a self-serving, self-dealing source of little or no employment about fifteen years ago—on national television. But there it is still—large sign, big office, patronage employees still at their desks—pretending to provide employment and training for a new generation of decent and desperate job-seekers.

States compete with one another for a shrinking pool of jobs and development opportunities, just as Jersey City has competed with lower Manhattan for office towers and apartment blocks that now stand half-empty, exempt from most taxes, an anchor around the neck of the city for the next twenty years. Within states, counties compete with counties, towns with towns, community colleges with community colleges, private universities with one another. Most of the governmental levers that people still pull—local economic development agencies, business improvement districts, big-bang development schemes such as ball fields and Olympic venues—do not match up to the breadth and depth of the problems to be solved.

If the nearly $800 billion in stimulus money is poured into these political operations and programmatic systems—new wine into old skins—then much of it will be wasted. Though Barack Obama has spent much less time as an organizer than as a lawyer, law professor, nonfiction writer, Illinois politician, and national politician, he is now facing a challenge that the organizer in him may be best equipped to confront. For instance, if he thinks like an organizer, he will understand that every dollar that runs through the most worrisome of his cabinet selections, Transportation Secretary Ray LaHood, should be monitored from day one. LaHood is a favorite of what *Chicago Tribune* columnist John Kass calls "the combine"—the bipartisan group of well-connected pols who own the public arena in Illinois and work hard to keep others out.

The president can be even tougher on the old political culture. He could direct his cabinet appointees to withhold funds from any municipality—like the hundreds in Illinois or New Jersey or New York—where public figures are allowed to have multiple jobs (for example, serving as a school superintendent and a paid state legislator), milk multiple salaries, and collect multiple pensions. Once the self-dealers divest themselves of multiple salaries and benefits, once they trim down to one paycheck for one job, then the federal money should flow.

The administration can use the stimulus money to end practices like these and reshape the delivery of public services throughout the country. Or it can rationalize these petty corruptions as the products of local decisions, best left in the hands of generational hacks in every city and county from Chicago to Camden, from Detroit to DuPage. These inbred and tightly knit cultures know how to resist and frustrate Ivy League lawyers and policy wonks. And they remain unmoved by compelling argument and soaring rhetoric. Until now, only relentless prosecutors could hold them accountable—*after* they had stolen funds and exploited public programs. The president can deal with this extraordinarily broad and deep corrosion *preemptively.* He and his allies—our Metro IAF organizations among them—could devise new ways to solve social issues that previous administrations, both Republican and Democratic, have failed to address.

When I think of the mismatch between problem and response that will undoubtedly arise if the administration does not take steps to sideline venal locals, I think of my late uncle, Nick Juric—someone who spent his life thinking creatively about solutions. Nick came to the United States with his Croatian parents at age six. He, his wife Babe, and their daughter lived a block away from us on Avers Avenue. We were one family in two houses, with my grandmother living with us on Ferdinand Street, and everyone in and out of either house at any time.

Nick and Babe ran a grocery for a while. Like our tavern, it never made it. After his business tanked,

Nick found a job at Ohmite Electronics, a facility in Skokie, just north of Chicago. Although a man of limited education—Nick did not even graduate high school—he was incredibly gifted both socially and mechanically. Soon, he was the senior manager of the plant of 300 electronics workers. He was a low-key and positive person who became president of the Croatian-American Club, head of the Holy Name Society, and a kind of jack-of-all-trades leader in his parish and ethnic community.

But his special genius was problem solving. As a youngster, I would watch him take on challenges. He would not react right away. He would spend what seemed like an eternity in thought. Eventually he would disappear into his basement workshop—first on Avers Avenue, then on Narragansett in Harwood Heights—and rummage aimlessly around, or so it seemed. He was trying to figure out whether he had the right tool to fix the problem.

If he did not have the right tool, he would try to *design and make it.*

I realized most of this only in retrospect.

It was almost anti-climactic when he surfaced with a fix. Most of the hard work had already been done in the period of thinking, searching downstairs, smoking a cigar on the porch for a while, sometimes inventing the tool that fit the problem. The implementation was the inevitable last stage of a process that started a few hours or a few days or a few weeks before. If he did not have an answer to a particularly thorny or specialized problem, which was very rare, he would invite over someone who did, and watch for hours on end as his guest confronted the challenge. The next time around, Nick would not need anyone's help.

We have a society loaded with the institutional equivalents of crooked doors, rusting pipes, leaky roofs, and creaking floors and foundations, but we have very little of what Nick Juric brought to his household and his workplace: the confidence required to stop and think; the patience to rummage around and reexamine the equipment already at hand and the judgment to decide what works; and, least of all, the skill to design and build a new and different tool that enables efficient problem-solving.

So, what are some new tools? Well, one is the newly reemergent small school—public, public charter, or religious. As I described in Chapter 2, in big cities such as Chicago, New York, and Philadelphia, innovative school leaders are looking at the unique set of challenges facing their communities and devising the tools to respond. Patience and distance. The political and bureaucratic apparatus should leave well enough alone. Do not interfere. Do not try to dominate. Do not stifle. Do not exploit. Do not obstruct. Do not hurry. The best of the people starting these schools and pouring their lives into them are like Nick. They looked at all the existing options and educational implements and decided that they did not match up to the current challenge. So they went into the workshop and fashioned—are fashioning—something new and different. Let them. And do not kid yourself that their successes are too local, too diffuse, too "anecdotal." This is the way real, lasting change happens. This is the way the American high school emerged in the early decades of its phenomenal 75-year run. Not from the top down. Not as a result of a single charismatic leader or national legislative act. But from the bottom up, locally owned, thoroughly tested, consistently perfected.

A second tool is perspective. The Midwest should see itself as the equivalent of a state in the European Union. In fact, when I described to my brilliant British colleague Bernadette Farrell how the United States is composed of regions with very distinct cultures, histories, challenges, and tensions, she said, simply, "Sounds like Europe." Maybe we are more like Europe now than we would like to admit. The Midwest might begin to see itself, think of itself, and operate at times as an ad hoc single state in the process of long-term reconstruction, as Germany did after World War II.

The universities of the Midwest would stop competing with one another, each offering similar math or science or computer or business courses. Instead, each university would specialize in one or several fields and become a national and international leader in that field. Maybe computer science in central and southern Illinois. Maybe math in Ohio. Maybe medical technology and nurse training in northern Illinois, Wisconsin, and Indiana.

The region as a whole could become the international center for elementary and secondary teacher training. Teaching apprenticeships and internships in its public systems would be rigorous and highly valued.

The federal government would offer massive block grants—in the billions of dollars—to regions that devise cooperative strategies of high impact. The metrics for success would be simple: first, the number of Americans who acquire the skills and tools to be effective, wage-earning professionals in a variety of essential fields; and, second, the number of paying foreign students attracted to the same set of programs. These foreign students would either remain in the

United States and contribute to our pool of human capital, or return to their home countries and build or rebuild their societies there.

A third tool would be, at the very least, a regional "skunkworks" devoted to retrofitting all American apartment buildings—high-end, middle-class, moderately subsidized, and public—with the boilers, windows, electrical systems, and plumbing improvements that would guarantee at least two more generations of useful life and would dramatically cut their energy use and energy costs. A skunkworks is the process used by the federal government and major corporations when they want to make a breakthrough in new technologies, often for defense. A top group of scientists and engineers—35 Nick Jurics—are recruited into a team and sent away from the agency or corporate headquarters, perhaps to some converted garage in San Jose. Removed from the bureaucracy, uninterrupted by fax or phone for the most part, these thinkers collectively grapple with the challenge placed before them.

In many ways this thinking has already been done by the best housing and technical assistance team in the nation: the Community Preservation Corporation in New York. But they need to begin translating their plans into action, and testing and experimenting will take time. Of course, the benefits of a skunk works are obvious. In the Northeast there are millions of units of housing, built before and after World War II, that would benefit from retrofitting and rehabilitation in order to cut energy costs, improve environmental conditions, and generate large-scale employment. In New York City alone, there are 1.6 million such units. The entities that design, perfect, and implement this rehabilitation—public, private, third-sector—should be encouraged and rewarded. The cities and public-housing agencies that most successfully advance this movement should also receive bonuses. There are new markets, new job opportunities, new and sustained benefits inherent in this third tool.

Everyone seems to mention and perhaps agree on the fourth tool—nationwide infrastructure repair—

but that should be cause for worry. An infrastructure strategy should be grounded in a larger strategy. And that larger strategy should revolve around the reinforcement and revival of institutions that create social and human capital—schools being one. About the same time the 75-year career of high school and human capital expansion peaked and began to decline, the long period characterized by systematic savings also stalled and went into reverse. So did the practice of building and renovating much of our infrastructure. The wave of renovation and upgrading that should have occurred, starting in the mid 1970s, never started. As a result, the water in many Baltimore City schools is undrinkable. Bottled water prevents the adults and children from getting sick. In a world of choices, even when a trillion dollars will be spent, replacing the pipes in Baltimore schools should take precedence. And only a critical mass of targeted economic and social gains will create the chain reaction that ensures other improvements will be achieved without permanent government stimulation.

These choices will not be easy, however logical they appear on the merits. As the economy shrinks, those with patronage jobs at all levels will hold on tighter. The transportation secretary may feel more at home with road builders and their lobbyists, not school renovators and water engineers. If we somehow choose to invest in better schools rather than more prisons, the prison industry will mobilize. Corrections unions, construction interests, lawyers, and bond counsels who make fortunes off prison expansion; towns and counties desperate for the prison industry as a source of employment; and politicians beholden to these interests or wedded to a tough-on-crime elctoral strategy will all rise up and defend the source of their power and influence.

No city mayor or county political operative will want federal money awarded in a way that reduces his or her power. The late Mayor Richard J. Daley taught many presidents that lesson. If President Johnson wanted Daley's electoral support, all federal money had to go through the mayor, not directly to local anti-poverty or community-development efforts independent of the machine. But that has meant that no solution not in the interest of a dominant mayor and suffocating machine can live and breathe.

In every area, with the exception of the new school revitalization, this centralization of money in the hands of politicians has stifled innovation and experimentation. The demolition of 18,000 units of Chicago public housing was supposed to generate subsidies that would provide replacement housing for the tenants who were displaced with a pat on the back and a Section 8 voucher in their hands. Only a few thousand units have been built in the more than ten years since, according to an exhaustive study by the *Chicago Tribune*. Approximately 600, by our estimate, are affordable. The market units that were supposed to generate subsidies for the affordable units are themselves not selling. And local foundations had to come up with a futile scheme to offer $10,000 incentives to people who would buy one of the overpriced structures. This is a typical Daley-era solution—disastrous for the poor and working poor; a subsidy eater, not a subsidy generator; and papered over by an extensive network of public and private public-relations firms.

Obstructionism will not end with the politicians and their enablers, of course. Colleges and universities also will not want to cooperate; will not want to choose one set of specialties over another; will not want to admit that they are better at a few things, but not nearly as good as their peers at others. Their leadership will not want to confront the heads of backwater academic departments, will not want to fight the hardest of all fights—the internal ones.

But these are the very struggles that must take place if we are to break out as a nation, a set of regions, from our current crisis and emerge stronger and more productive than we are today. And it is the test of strength that our young national administration is already facing and will face until its last hour in office. It is also a test for a new generation of citizens'-power organizations like EBC and Baltimoreans

United In Leadership Development, Greater Boston Interfaith Organization, and United Power for Action and Justice in Cook County. They understand power, how to wield it, how to engage it, how to outmaneuver people who are also practiced in its use. They are essential new players in the realignment of interests and institutions that will need to take place to bring real progress to these efforts.

A MONTH AGO, WHILE IN LONDON WORKING with the groups affiliated with the IAF of the United Kingdom—the Citizens Organising Foundation— my wife and I took a trip north to see Hadrian's Wall. We had read about it in Derek Williams's book, *Romans and Barbarians*, and had harbored a decade-long dream to see it and to walk along it.

The day we arrived there, near the Scottish border, was brilliantly sunny, with a brisk wind and cool temperatures. We stopped at Corbridge, where the Romans built a settlement a few miles south of the wall, then went to the Chesters, along the Tyne

River, where we walked through the fort and down to the remains of the baths near the banks of the river. Then we drove further west to Housesteads, one of the great remaining forts, with portions of the original wall ranging east and west, up and down ruggedly steep slopes. To the north, beyond the spongy valley and remaining forests, was Scotland. From that direction, the "barbarians" of the second and third centuries, their bodies and faces painted blue, stormed these walls and attacked these settlements. The settlements themselves were defended by Roman troops conscripted in Belgium and other corners of earlier Roman conquest. By the fourth century, the Romans had withdrawn. This attempt at partition and containment, like so many others, ended badly. With the wind whipping across hills and stones, with sheep grazing along the ramparts, the tribes barely noticed the barrier after a time.

As a monument to past imperial ambition, it is magnificent and even understandable. In this bare, remote, often-brutal world, with so much of both the landscape and life uncertain and threatening, the notion of a physical barrier, of strong troops stationed along the entire waist of Britain and cavalry nearby ready to respond—the whole enterprise had its powerful internal logic. We could see it and sense it nearly 2,000 years later. This method of control kept conquered regions busy—slaves building walls; allied soldiers manning the ramparts, far away from Rome, where their presence could not contribute to the ongoing civil strife.

The new walls we keep building along the Rio Grande and the prison fortresses we keep expanding in every state reflect this same logic.

Our deepening culture of insecurity, feeding a demand for new and more intrusive security systems and policies, depends on a sense of the negative, not the affirmative, individual. The expectation is that most people—particularly those who are poor and with whom those who are not poor are unfamiliar—most of the time, will do the wrong thing, if given the opportunity.

The response is the boundless American program of security, which hardens and expands a caste system built off a large and growing group of enemies—unwanted people who must be contained or kept out, dominated or defeated—and another large caste of security personnel. Guards; airport checkers; cops; private security companies, some larger than the armies of other nations; consultants; lobbyists; underwriters—the containers and the contained live and grow together.

This culture of insecurity depends on institutions that "succeed" by sequestering people from the larger society—consuming increasing portions of our shrinking public treasury to add to the inmate population. As these institutions become more powerful, they begin to operate on every part of society—even on the political leaders who helped create them but now want to limit them.

They promote a worldview that distracts people from the greater challenges of decline, a philosophy that shifts responsibility for that decline to outsiders or "others" and increases the status of those who demonize or manage these supposed threats. That means that the majority never has to take any direct or personal responsibility, never has to change its perspectives or patterns, never has to sacrifice or struggle or risk.

Is there real evil in the world? Of course. I grew up in a neighborhood where young men were recruited by the mob and murdered for fun or profit or both, where bars were blown up if their owners refused to pay off the racketeers and corrupt cops, where a school fire killed 95 people because of a neglectful Archdiocese that took 49 years to erect a rather sad monument to the dead and that did little to protect the children of fire survivors from the more recent sexual abuse scandal. For me, evil is not an abstract word in a philosophical or religious text. I've seen it, met it, felt it, and fought it. It must be checked, contained, or eliminated.

But the greater part of the world is still full of opportunities. Ronald Reagan famously said, "Mr. Gorbachev, tear down that wall." And we all cheered—the greater portion of our planet cheered—when the Berlin Wall finally fell.

We will cheer again as we decide to relate to, rather than dominate, our potential partners in the wider world.

We will cheer when we realign our priorities to equip young people for productive work and civic lives, rather than wasted decades in jails.

We will cheer when we commit ourselves, as our London colleagues have done, to turning strangers into citizens, to turning the marginal into members, not into pariahs or prisoners.

And we will cheer each time we remove the obstacles that make the race of life, in Lincoln's words, unfair, when all have a fair start and a clear path toward full participation in our economy and our society.

Maybe, then, our cities finally will stop smoldering. The smoke will clear. The sirens will grow silent. And our communities will ring with the sound of hammers and saws, so that, as Zechariah foretold, our seniors will sit on their stoops again, and our children will play safely in our streets.

BOSTON REVIEW BOOKS

Boston Review Books is an imprint of *Boston Review*, a bimonthly magazine of ideas. The book series, like the magazine, is animated by hope, committed to equality, and convinced that the imagination eludes political categories. Visit bostonreview.net for more information.